AMAZING SCIENCE
MATERIALS

Sally Hewitt

WAYLAND

Published in paperback in 2014 by Wayland
Copyright © 2014 Wayland

Hachette Children's Books
338 Euston Road
London
NW1 3BH

Senior Editor: Joyce Bentley
Senior Design Manager: Rosamund Saunders
Designer: Tall Tree

British Library Cataloguing in Publication Data
Hewitt, Sally,
    Materials - (Amazing Science)
    1. Materials - Juvenile literature
    I. Title
    620.1'1

ISBN-13: 978-0-7502-8059-4

Printed and bound in China

10 9 8 7 6 5 4 3 2 1

Cover photograph: Logger cutting down a tree in a forest with
a chain saw in USA, Alaska, Tongass National Forest.
Mark Kelley/Getty Images
Title page: Dorling Kindersley/Getty Images

Photo credits: AFP/Getty Images 6, Getty Images News 7,
Bridgeman Art Library/Getty Images 8, Estelle Rancurel/Getty
Images 9, Nick Greaves/Getty Images 10, Joseph Van Os/Getty
Images 11, Wes Walker/Getty Images 12, Nick Hawkes;
Ecoscene/Corbis 13, Corbis 14, Titus/Getty Images 15, Jim
Zukerman/Corbis 16, Joel Sartore/Getty Images 17, Mark
Kelley/Getty Images 18, Dorling Kindersley/Getty Images 19,
David Sanger Photography/Alamy 20, Nicola Tree/Getty Images
21, Tom & Dee Ann McCarthy/Corbis 22, Steve Satushek/Getty
Images 23, Arvind Garg/Getty Images 24, BE&W Agencja
Fotograficzna Sp. z o. o./Alamy 25, Jean-Paul
Pellssier/Reuters/Corbis 26 John Humble/Getty images 27.

Contents

Amazing materials

The Akashi Kaikyo bridge is made of steel and concrete. It can stand firm in strong winds and earthquakes.

Steel and concrete are kinds of materials. Materials are what things are made of.

Bricks, plastic, glass, and metal are some of the materials we use every day.

The walls of this house are made of strong bricks.

YOUR TURN!

Collect small things such as pencils, toys, buttons and coins. Find out what materials they are made of.

What is a solid?

This statue is made of a strong, solid stone called marble. It looks almost new but it is nearly 2,000 years old.

Solid materials like marble have a shape of their own.

You are solid. A chair is solid and so is a book.

A solid chair holds you up when you sit on it.

YOUR TURN!

Put some solid objects in a bag. Try to guess what the objects are just by feeling their shape.

SCIENCE WORDS: solid shape

What is a liquid?

A huge amount of water pours over the Victoria Falls every second. Water is always moving and changing shape.

Some materials, such as water, are liquids. Liquids take on the shape of the container they are in.

Water doesn't have a shape of its own.

YOUR TURN!

Collect jugs, mugs and bottles. Pour water from one to the other. See the water take the shape of the container.

Water can be solid. It can freeze into an iceberg.

SCIENCE WORDS: liquid container

What is a gas?

Hot air fills a balloon and lifts it high into the sky. The hot air takes the shape of the balloon.

Air is a kind of gas. Gas is a material that moves and changes shape.

You can't see air but you need air to live.

Smoke is a kind of gas. It changes shape as it moves.

YOUR TURN!

Your breath is a kind of gas. Blow up a balloon. Watch your breath take the shape of the balloon.

SCIENCE WORDS: gas   air

Changing shape

A potter shapes a lump of clay into a pot. The soft wet clay is baked hard in a kiln.

Some materials can be squashed and stretched into different shapes.

You can squash, stretch and change the shape of soft dough. It goes hard when it is cooked.

You can cut bread to change its shape.

YOUR TURN!

Make a clay model. Let it dry hard. How can you change its shape now?

SCIENCE WORDS: **soft hard change kiln**

Melting and moulding

Diggers and cranes moulded from metal are hard at work. Metal is a strong material for tough jobs.

Metal is found in rocks in the ground.
Iron and gold are kinds of metal.

Very hot metal melts and becomes a
liquid. It is poured into a container
called a mould.

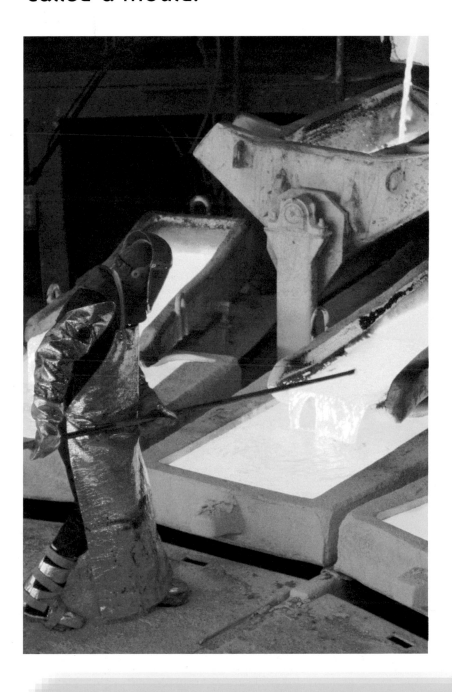

When liquid metal
cools, it hardens
into the shape of
the mould.

YOUR TURN!

*Ask an adult to help you
make jelly. When liquid jelly
cools it takes on the shape
of the jelly mould.*

SCIENCE WORDS: melt   metal   mould

Wood and paper

A huge tree can take hundreds of years to grow. It can be cut down for its wood in a few minutes.

Wood is a natural material. It can be cut with tools to make things.

Wood can be chopped into small pieces, mixed with water and pressed to make paper.

YOUR TURN!

Fold a piece of paper into a paper dart. Throw it and watch it fly.

You can fold, cut and write on paper.

SCIENCE WORDS: cut fold

Glass

This sparkling glass was once dry sand. Glass is a hard material but it breaks easily.

Sand is heated with other materials to make glass.

Light shines through glass. It is transparent which means you can see through it.

Windows are made of flat sheets of glass.

YOUR TURN!

Find things that are made of glass. Why do you think they are made of glass?

SCIENCE WORDS: **glass break transparent**

Plastic

A small child can pick up a big toy fire engine. The fire engine is light because it is made of plastic.

Plastic is a material made in a factory. It can be moulded into all kinds of shapes.

Water doesn't soak through plastic because it is a waterproof material.

YOUR TURN!

Pour water on different materials. Which materials are waterproof?

A plastic coat, boots and an umbrella keep you dry in the rain.

SCIENCE WORDS: plastic light waterproof

23

Cloth

A worm made the silk that these saris are made from. Silk worms spin threads which make the silk.

Silk, cotton and wool are natural materials. Cotton comes from a plant and wool comes from sheep.

Cloth is cut and sewn to make clothes.

A teddy is made of soft cloth. A toy car is made of tough plastic.

YOUR TURN!

Collect pieces of different kinds of cloth. Stick them onto card to make a picture or pattern.

SCIENCE WORDS: cloth silk wool cotton

Recycled materials

This piece of art is made of empty plastic bottles. They have been used again instead of being thrown away.

Things that are used again are recycled.

Plastic, paper and metal are materials that can be recycled and made into something new.

Waste paper can be recycled to make more paper.

YOUR TURN!

Don't waste materials. Recycle paper, plastic and tins instead of throwing them away.

SCIENCE WORDS: recycled   waste

Glossary

Air
A gas all around us that we can't see.

Change
When you change something, you make it different.

Cloth
Cloth is made by weaving or knitting threads together.

Container
A box, a bottle or a jug used to hold things.

Cotton
The fibres of some plants that are used to make fabric and other products.

Cut
We use a sharp tool such as a knife or scissors to cut bread, paper or cloth into smaller pieces.

Fold
To bend something flat, such as paper or cloth, without breaking or cutting it.

Gas
A material that moves and changes shape. Air is a kind of gas.

Glass
A material that you can see through and that breaks easily. Windows are made of glass.

Hard
Things that are hard are difficult to cut, bend or break.

Light
Things that are light do not weigh very much. Light is the opposite of heavy.

Liquid
Liquid materials flow and don't have a shape of their own.

Made
Things that are made are not natural. They are made in a factory or by hand.

Materials
Materials are what things are made of. Paper, wood and plastic are kinds of materials.

Melt
To change something from a solid to a liquid by heating it.

Metal
A material found in the ground. Iron and gold are kinds of metal.

Mould
A shaped container. Liquid is poured into a mould and left to harden into the shape of the mould.

Plastic
Plastic is not a natural material. It is made in a factory.

Recycled
Things that are recycled have been used again.

Shape
The outline of something.

Silk
A fine cloth of silk threads made by silkworms.

Soft
Soft things feel smooth and are easily squashed or bent.

Solid
Things that are solid have their own shape.

Transparent
You can see through transparent material. Glass is transparent.

Waste
You waste something when you throw it away instead of using it again.

Waterproof
Waterproof material keeps out water. Raincoats are made of waterproof material.

Wool
A material made from the woolly coat of a sheep.

Index